BIOFEEDBACK

BIOFEEDBACK

FACT OR FAD?

BY ANN E. WEISS

A GROLIER COMPANY

FRANKLIN WATTS
NEW YORK / LONDON / TORONTO / SYDNEY / 1984
AN IMPACT BOOK

FOR JANE HELLEGERS,
FRIEND AND LIBRARIAN

Photographs courtesy of: AP/Wide World: p. 5;
The Bettmann Archive, Inc.: pp. 15, 45;
The Menninger Foundation: pp. 25, 26;
UPI: pp. 31, 57, 68, 78;
The Rockefeller University, Ingbert Grüttner: p. 50.

Library of Congress Cataloging in Publication Data

Weiss, Ann E., 1943-
Biofeedback, fact or fad?

(An Impact book)
Bibliography: p.
Includes index.
Summary: Explores the science of "biofeedback" and
describes the use of biofeedback techniques to help
humans solve medical and psychological problems. Also
discusses the future implications of biofeedback training.
1. Biofeedback training—Juvenile literature.
[1. Biofeedback training] I. Title.
RC489.B53W45 1984   615.8'51   84-5808
ISBN 0-531-04851-9

CONTENTS

BIOFEEDBACK

1

"WILD DREAMS OF THE FUTURE"

The patient, a middle-aged woman, had been severely injured in an automobile accident. A major facial nerve had been severed, and the woman was unable to move any part of the left side of her face. She could not close or blink her left eye.

Surgeons lost no time in trying to help. Locating the undamaged portion of the facial nerve, they skillfully sutured it to a nerve running through the woman's big neck-shoulder muscle. Now, just by twitching her shoulder, the patient could blink her eye and move her face.

But her facial movements had little resemblance to natural movements. Any time the shoulder nerve was activated, her face moved. The result was a wildly fluttering eyelid—a face that rippled in a series of convulsive tics. Worst of all, the two sides of the woman's face seemed to move independently of each other. The movements of the damaged left side were not synchronized with those of the undamaged right.

How to correct these problems? The woman decided to try biofeedback training.

Electrodes—disc-shaped devices capable of picking up

and registering tiny electrical impulses—were placed on the injured part of her face. Wires linked these electrodes to an electromyograph (EMG), a machine that measures and records electrical changes in the muscles. Connected to the EMG was an oscilloscope—a small screen, somewhat like a television screen.

Each muscle movement in a human or an animal produces a very small electrical change in the muscle cells. Every time the woman's face moved, her muscle cells sent an electrical signal through the electrodes and into the EMG. There the signal was recorded and amplified—made stronger and clearer.

At the same time, the amplified signal was converted into a flash of light. Each flash appeared on the screen. Together, a series of flashes made a quickly changing pattern. By watching this pattern closely, the woman could tell how her face was moving. She could also remember exactly what she had done to her muscles to cause those movements. Her job was to try to put cause and effect together, to "learn" to control her facial muscles.

But there was more to the woman's biofeedback training than that. The screen showed her *two* patterns of flashing lights. The first was the one she herself produced. The second was the pattern that would be produced by normal, undamaged facial nerves and muscles. The woman had to try to make her pattern as much like the normal pattern as possible.

It was no easy task. The training went on for months. Slowly, the woman strengthened her facial muscles. She "trained" the muscles in her shoulder to produce only those facial movements that she wanted them to produce. Finally, she learned to work the two sides of her face together in synchronous movement.

A second biofeedback trainee, a young New York City advertising copywriter, had an entirely different problem. This woman had suffered a brain hemorrhage and was partly paralyzed. Besides that she had high blood pressure—hypertension. Although she was on medication for the high blood pressure, it did not seem to be doing much good. Doctors warned her that her hypertension could contribute to further medical problems in the future. When the woman learned that biofeedback might help her lower her blood pressure, her doctors agreed that she should try it.

During training sessions, the woman's blood pressure had to be constantly monitored. A cuff was wrapped around her arm, and readings began to be taken. The woman was instructed to sit back, to relax, and just to *think* about bringing her blood pressure down. Each time the machine showed that it had dipped below a certain point, she would hear a beeping tone. The woman was told to try to produce that beep as often as possible—to "learn" to lower her blood pressure.

That is what she did. The weeks went by, and the young woman's hypertension lessened. Doctors took her off medication—and her blood pressure continued to drop. Soon, the delighted patient was off on a two-week vacation in the Caribbean, a vacation that would have been impossible before her biofeedback training.

Compared to life-threatening high blood pressure and a disfiguring tic, an occasional tension headache might not seem much of a problem. But to the businessman who had the headaches, they were serious indeed. They were painful and they frequently interfered with his work. Could biofeedback help him get rid of the headaches? He decided to give it a try.

At each training session, the businessman was seated in a quiet, darkened room. Electrodes were attached to his forehead. They were linked at the other end to an electromyograph like the one used by the first patient. In this case, though, the EMG was designed to translate electrical charges into sound, rather than into light.

Sitting in the dim room, the man heard a rapid series of clicks. These were signals that his forehead muscles were giving off many tiny charges—an indication that the muscles there were tight and tense. Such tightness, doctors know, can help bring about a headache.

Consciously, following his trainer's instructions, the man tried to relax. He was rewarded by a slowing down of the clicking sound. After only a few sesssions, he had "learned" to prevent his headaches. No more aspirin for him!

No more tranquilizers, either. Elated by his success with biofeedback, the man decided to use the same technique to learn the secret of deep relaxation. He would learn to put himself into an "alpha state."

"Alpha" refers to a certain kind of electrical pattern emitted by the brain. It is a pattern that many scientists believe is associated with feelings of peace and tranquility. A number of biofeedback researchers claim that they can train people to produce relaxing alpha waves whenever they want to. We'll examine this claim—and the methods the researchers use—in detail in Chapter 4.

In fact, our patient did learn to put himself into an alpha state, a condition that some who have experienced it call a "mindless euphoria." Others liken it to a kind of drug-free "high."

Can biofeedback really replace aspirin and tranquilizers? Allow people to throw away their blood pressure medicine? Permit them to manipulate nerves and muscles

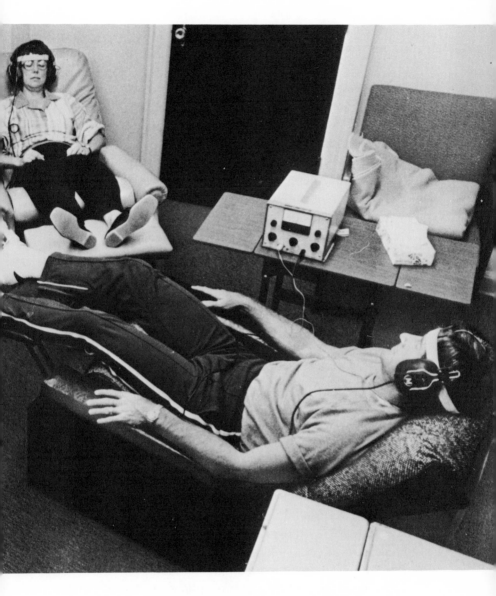

*These students are learning biofeedback
techniques in a training session
at the Menninger Foundation clinic.*

deep within the body—so deep within that most people are not even aware that they exist?

A number of men and women researching biofeedback today are convinced that the answers to such questions are *yes*. They claim that they have used biofeedback techniques to successfully treat a wide range of conditions, from high blood pressure to asthma, from migraine headache to ulcers, from stuttering to cancer. Biofeedback can even help the paralyzed to learn to walk again, and the deaf to speak, some researchers say. Others believe that biofeedback can be used to increase creativity and to improve mental health.

One pioneer in the field, Dr. Barbara B. Brown, has described the attitude of enthusiastic visitors to her laboratory at the Veterans' Administration Hospital in Sepulveda, California: "It was as if they felt suddenly confronted by the impossible dream, a panacea for all time and for all things."

An eternal, universal cure-all? Many doubt that biofeedback is any such thing. Its promise is a false promise, they say. Claims made for it have been exaggerated. True, it can help people like our first patient to retrain diseased or damaged nerves and muscles. But for most others, the results of biofeedback training are small or nonexistent.

Even when there are results, the skeptics say, those results are likely to be only temporary. Our second patient, for example, returned from her Caribbean vacation with extremely elevated blood pressure. She went back on her medication at once—and stayed on it. For headache victims, too, initial good results may not last.

Dr. Brown herself counsels a degree of caution. When those excited visitors poured into her lab, she points out, "biofeedback was just being born." Much basic research remained to be done. "There was none of the conventional, hard scientific evidence actually down on paper to warrant the wild dreams of the future," Dr. Brown wrote.

That was in 1974. Today the situation is much the same. There are those with "wild dreams" for biofeedback. But much research is yet to be done.

2

WIGGLING EARS AND MOTIONLESS RATS

In a sense, biofeedback began with ear wiggling. But what is biofeedback?

Biofeedback is feedback plus biology. We use the word "feedback" to describe the way a system regulates itself by using part of its output as input. Or, as the mathematician and electronics innovator Norbert Wiener expressed it, feedback is "a method of controlling a system by reinserting into it the results of its past performance."

All of us are familiar with feedback systems in everyday life. A furnace, for instance, is linked to a feedback device called a thermostat. The thermostat is set to a certain temperature—68 degrees Fahrenheit, perhaps. A thermometer in the thermostat constantly measures the temperature of the room. When that temperature dips below 68 degrees, a device within the thermostat sends an electrical signal to the motor of the furnace. That signal activates a switch in the motor, and the furnace turns on. Heat flows through the room. As the temperature rises again to 68 degrees, the fact is registered in the thermostat. Back goes another signal. The furnace shuts down.

Air conditioners employ similar feedback "loops." So do electric ovens, clothes dryers, and hundreds of other machines.

Sometimes, human beings become part of a feedback system. The driver of a car, approaching a curve, begins to turn the steering wheel. The car responds, but the driver is aware that it's not turning fast enough. Another tug on the wheel. Whoops! Too hard. The driver feels the tires begin to skid and makes a quick, new adjustment. The driver controls the car's steering mechanism, and feedback allows that control to be precise.

Automatic feedback systems are all around us—and within us, as well. Sniff the delicious odor of a baking pizza. Immediately, salivary glands inside your mouth begin producing the moisture that will allow you to swallow smoothly and easily. Other parts of your digestive system, receiving the information that food may be on the way, are activated.

Thousands—possibly millions—of other body systems work on a feedback principle. Our five senses—sight, hearing, taste, smell, and touch—collect information from the outside world. Nerves carry that information to the brain, where it is stored and used. Sometimes the information is put to use at once. Put your hand on a hot stove and the feedback is instant: Move your hand! Overeat, and feedback comes more slowly, in the form of the growing discomfort of an upset stomach. Perspiring, sneezing, itching, and scratching are other examples of natural feedback control systems.

The body's feedback systems help us to live safely and comfortably in our surroundings. They provide the signals that tell our body systems when it's time to speed up or to slow down, to start or to stop. Natural feedback enables us to change and adapt as the environment around us changes.

And the great thing about this is that it works automatically, without our even thinking about it. A person doesn't have to plan to salivate, or to activate the digestive tract, upon picking up a slice of pizza. The digestive system works all by itself. So does the circulatory system that sends blood pumping out from the heart into all parts of the body. So do dozens of other systems. Altogether, these systems are under the control of what is known as the involuntary, or *autonomic,* nervous system.

People, and animals, have a voluntary nervous system, too. Scientists refer to it as the central nervous system. It controls all of our so-called voluntary actions. Walking, sitting, raising a hand to catch a baseball—all are examples of voluntary muscular actions. All are controlled by the central nervous system. All involve the use of skeletal muscles, muscles that are attached to the bone.

The two nervous systems, voluntary and autonomic, are completely separate. Living creatures make conscious decisions to control voluntary functions. But they cannot "decide" to control autonomic functions. At least that is what virtually all Western scientists—Europeans and Americans—have generally assumed.

In other parts of the world, assumptions are different. In the nations of the East, a few men and women have claimed that they could use their minds to control the involuntary systems within their bodies. For example, yogis—Indian religious mystics—maintained that they could speed their rate of heartbeat—or slow it down. One said he could produce a ten-degree difference between the temperature of his thumb and that of his little finger. Another claimed to be able to slow his breathing to just one or two breaths a minute over a period of several hours. This is well below the rate of respiration that normally activates an involuntary reflex. That reflex compels a person to gasp in deep rapid breaths, whether he or she wants to or not in order not to suffocate.

Millions of their countrymen and women had no trouble believing the yogis, but to Western minds, the claims sounded ridiculous. The mystics must be resorting to trickery, Western scientists said. The feats they said they could perform were too far outside the boundaries of Western medicine and psychology to seem believable. Those boundaries rested on the firm conviction that mind and body are, and must forever be, separate and distinct. That is, until experiments in the wiggling of the ears began to cast doubt on that conviction.

It was an American psychologist, J. H. Blair, who first investigated ear wiggling in the interests of science. He reported on his experiments in a professional journal, *Psychological Review*, in 1901.

Blair's aim was to discover how people develop voluntary control over the movements of their muscles. He chose to work with ears, because people do not use their ear muscles. Unlike dogs, foxes, and other wild animals, human beings do not rely heavily upon a sense of hearing to detect enemies and hidden dangers. As a result, they do not need to move or "cock" their ears to pick up faint sounds. Over the ages, people have lost the ability to move their ears at will.

Could they learn the skill? Blair gathered a group of young men, his experimental "subjects." He attached electrodes to their ears and gave each subject a mild shock. That shock caused their ears to wiggle.

Next, the men tried to move their ears without receiving the shock. Each remembered how it had felt when his ears *had* moved. Now, by tensing this or that large group of muscles—around the mouth, in the forehead—they tried to recapture that feeling. When they succeeded, their ears moved.

Gradually, the men's skill improved. They learned to distinguish those tiny muscle contractions that caused ear movement from the larger contractions that meant a clenched jaw or a furrowed brow. Before long, for anyone interested in the sight of serene-faced young men with twitching ears, J. H. Blair's lab was definitely the place to be.

Blair did not invent biofeedback, and today his name is largely forgotten. But he did employ several ideas and techniques of modern biofeedback. He was concerned with learning, with teaching muscles to accomplish new and unfamiliar tasks. Furthermore, he suspected that to control a response, a person must be able to sense that response. His young men needed to know how it felt to wiggle their ears before they could learn to do it at will. That is why he first gave each one the electric shock. That shock let the men know what was expected of them. Feedback from their own facial muscles told them when they were manipulating those muscles in the right direction.

The experiments Blair designed and carried out were interesting and successful, but other scientists did not follow up on them. It was to be nearly sixty years before the next scientific ear wiggler came along.

He was also an American, Dr. Neal E. Miller. At the time he decided to learn to wiggle his ears, Miller was a professor of psychology at Yale University in New Haven, Connecticut. He later moved to Rockefeller University in New York City.

Actually, the task that Miller set himself was more difficult than the one Blair had given his subjects. Miller could already wiggle both of his ears in unison. He wanted to learn to wiggle each one separately. He began practice sessions in front of the bathroom mirror.

Miller had a reason for using the mirror. Like Blair, he believed that sensing a response is essential to controlling that response. So he watched himself closely as he attempted to wiggle just one ear. Each time he caught a glimpse of independent movement—even the tiniest movement—he grinned and congratulated himself. That congratulation was his "reward" for another step taken toward his goal.

Although Neal Miller's experiment may sound frivolous, it was anything but. In his university lab, the eminent psychologist was deep into research about learning and how it takes place. He had some unorthodox ideas about both.

The orthodox, or traditional, idea was that two types of learning are possible for animals as well as for humans. One kind involves responses controlled by the autonomic nervous system.

A Russian scientist, Ivan Petrovich Pavlov, did the classic experiments on autonomic learning nearly 100 years ago. In the first stage of the experiment, Pavlov placed a hungry dog in a cage. Food, in the form of powdered meat, was placed on the dog's tongue. The dog salivated.

In the experiment's second stage, Pavlov fed the hungry, salivating dog as before. But this time, just before feeding, a bell was rung.

In the final stage, there was no feeding, only the sound of a bell. But the dog salivated just the same. A part of its autonomic nervous system had "learned" that the bell meant food. It had become "conditioned" to associate food and bell. The dog's digestive system responded to the noise just as it would have responded to food itself. In 1904, Pavlov received a Nobel prize in physiology and medicine for his work in "classical conditioning."

*The Russian scientist
Ivan Petrovich Pavlov,
demonstrates his experiment
in conditioning.*

The second type of animal and human learning is called "operant conditioning." It involves the voluntary nervous system.

A psychologist named B. F. Skinner has done much of the basic work on operant conditioning. Skinner is a professor emeritus of psychology at Harvard University in Cambridge, Massachusetts. In a typical Skinner experiment, a hungry, thirsty pigeon is placed in a cage. Outside the cage are bowls of food and water.

Frantically, the pigeon flutters about the cage, trying to get at the bowls. By accident, it brushes up against a small lever. The lever moves, allowing the cage door to open. The pigeon eats and drinks.

Over and over, the procedure is repeated. As the days pass, the pigeon learns to associate pushing the lever with getting food and water. Eventually, it works the lever automatically as soon as it is placed in the cage. It has learned how to operate to get its reward.

Skinner's pigeons, and other animals he has worked with, have learned some fancy tricks. Rats run through complicated mazes to get food—or to avoid the "punishment" of a painful electric shock. Cats pull at loops of string or press on bars to operate doors and windows for the same purposes. Birds pick out simple tunes on electric keyboards.

For most Western psychologists in the late 1950s, the differences between operant and classical conditioning were clear and sharp. Operant conditioning involved body systems that an animal could control at will. It could "decide" to use its muscles to move a lever, enter a particular passageway in a maze, or push a bar. In operant conditioning, an animal works to get a reward or to avoid a punishment. We use the principles of operant conditioning when we teach a dog to beg for food or when we work to perfect a tennis stroke.

Classical conditioning is another matter. It involves systems that scientists assumed to be beyond the conscious control of man or animal. It is a method of "training" glands, nerve cells, blood vessels, and such internal muscles as those of the heart or intestine. Rewards and punishments were not believed to be relevant in classical conditioning. After all, how would you "reward" a heart for beating regularly? Or "punish" the intestines for doing an inefficient job of digesting a Thanksgiving Day dinner?

Neal Miller thought he knew just how. Over the years, he had come to question the idea that there is a sharp, absolute distinction between the two types of learning. "Failing to see any clear-cut dichotomy" between voluntary and autonomic learning, Miller wrote in 1969, he "assumed there is only one kind of learning."

By the late 1950s, Miller was planning experiments to prove this assumption correct. Designing such experiments was difficult enough. A further problem was finding people who were willing to work with him as research assistants. Miller's ideas were so revolutionary that few young scientists wanted to be associated with them. They thought it might damage their professional careers later on.

Nevertheless, Miller did find some people to help, and he began experimenting. One of his first projects was to "teach" animals to speed up their digestion and to slow down their breathing. The results were inconclusive. Miller also made an attempt to "teach" rabbits to control the flow of blood through their ears. This experiment—which was unsuccessful—was later described by Miller as "harebrained."

Finally, Miller had a real success. In 1964 he set up a series of experiments involving thirsty dogs. The dogs were divided into two groups. The first group was to be "taught" to increase salivation; the second, to decrease it.

Salivation is an autonomic function. According to Western scientific tradition, its rate could not be affected by a system of rewards and punishments. But rewards and punishments were exactly what Miller offered the thirsty dogs.

The dogs in the first group were given water each time they produced saliva above a certain rate. Those in the second group got a drink only when their saliva production fell below that rate.

As the experiments continued, the dogs in each group performed just as Miller had hoped they would. The first group salivated more, and the second salivated less. The animals had "learned" voluntary control of an involuntary function.

Or had they? The results were still not conclusive. Critics charged that the dogs had not really learned to control their salivary glands. Instead, they had learned to manipulate certain skeletal muscles near those glands. Activating those muscles in particular ways could have allowed the dogs to speed up salivation, or to slow it down. In other words, the dogs might have learned a voluntary muscular response rather than an involuntary glandular one.

To answer this criticism, Miller designed another set of trials. It is upon these experiments that much of the theory behind the science of biofeedback has been based.

To demonstrate that voluntary and involuntary learning are one and the same, Miller knew that he would have to make sure that his experimental animals could not make use of any part of their voluntary nervous systems. They must not be able to employ any of the skeletal muscles controlled by that system. Only then—and only if he could get them to alter an autonomic function—would he have proved that the animals had learned voluntary control of an involuntary system.

To prevent the animals from using muscles under their voluntary control, Miller decided to paralyze them with an injection of *d*-tubocurarine. *D*-tubocurarine is a refined form of curare, the deadly "arrow poison" of some South American Indian tribes.

Of course, Dr. Miller did not plan to use curare in deadly amounts. He would use just enough to render his experimental animals—in this case, rats—immobile. Until the effects of the curare wore off, they would not even be able to breathe on their own. Respirators would do it for them. However, curare does not affect the muscles of the internal organs. That meant that the rats' hearts and their circulatory systems would continue to function normally. The drug does not affect mental awareness, either. The rats would be fully alert during the experiment.

Once the rats were paralyzed, Miller intended to "teach" them to change the rate of their heartbeats. One group would "learn" to speed the rate up, and the other would "learn" to slow it down.

But what to offer the rats as a reward? Paralyzed animals cannot eat or drink. So instead of using food or water, Miller decided to take advantage of the work done about ten years earlier by a pair of Canadian scientists. The two, James Olds and Peter Milner, had discovered the location of a "pleasure center" in the brain. Stimulating this center electrically produces pleasurable sensations in an animal. Miller chose such stimulation as a reward.

It took Miller and a research assistant, Jay Trowill, three years to solve all the problems involved in designing and setting up the new experiments. At last, they were ready to begin.

Electrodes were implanted in the pleasure centers of the rats' brains. The animals were paralyzed with *d*-tubo-curarine. Respirators were switched on. Monitors began recording the rats' heartbeats.

No animal has an entirely regular heartbeat. When the animal exercises vigorously, it speeds up, naturally. But even when an animal is at rest, tiny irregularities occur. Two beats may come slightly closer together than usual. A third is delayed by the tiniest fraction of a second, and so on.

The monitors Miller and Trowill used were sensitive enough to detect such irregularities. The rest of their equipment was sophisticated enough to send the rats quick rewards for those irregularities. The rats in the group that was supposed to increase heartbeat rate were rewarded—with a mild shock to the pleasure center— each time two heartbeats came unusually close together. Those in the group learning to decrease heartbeat rate were rewarded for each unusually slow heartbeat.

The experiments continued for some time. When they were over, in 1966, the rats in one group did have a faster-than-normal heartbeat rate. The rats in the other group had a slower-than-normal rate. The changes were small, but they did exist.

Rats in both groups had achieved voluntary control over an involuntary function. They had apparently done it with no help from skeletal muscles controlled by the central nervous system. They had done it with a system of rewards, rewards that also served as feedback to tell them when they were doing what the experimenters wanted them to do.

Throughout the rest of the 1960s, Miller and his associates performed other experiments aimed at confirming the results of the "curare experiments" and persuading the remaining skeptics to accept those results. They succeeded in getting one animal to slow its heart from 530 beats a minute to 230—an enormous change. They showed that the animals that "learned" to alter their heartbeats could "remember" what they had learned for at least as long as three months. Nor were the experiments limited to heartbeat. Miller caused one group of animals to speed up the rate at which they formed urine. A group of rats learned to increase blood circulation in just one ear at a time—to "blush" in one ear.

Taken together, the series of experiments by Miller and his assistants created a sensation in the scientific community. The experiments called into question one of the most deeply held beliefs of Western science, that of the total separation of voluntary and involuntary functions, of the sharp distinction between mind and body. They shed new light on the claims of Indian yogis and other Eastern mystics.

They also helped to fuel the growing biofeedback revolution.

3

MIRACLE CURES?

In the 1960s, while Dr. Neal Miller was conducting his experiments at Yale and Rockefeller universities, a man named Dr. Elmer Green and his wife and co-worker, Alyce, were carrying on a series of biofeedback experiments at the Menninger Foundation in Topeka, Kansas. They were teaching people to warm their hands.

The Greens had long been fascinated by psychophysiology—the study of the ways in which mind and body interact and influence each other. Biofeedback, they believed, was an ideal way to learn more about the science.

In their Topeka laboratory, the Greens seated would-be hand-warmers in a quiet, restful room. They attached electrodes to their fingers and wired the electrodes to meters that registered temperature changes. The Greens called the meters "temperature trainers." The temperature trainers were clearly visible to each subject.

The subjects' assignment was to try to get the meters to show an increase in finger temperature. Each brought his or her mental powers to bear on the task. Different people used different strategies to do this. One subject imagined herself wearing a pair of thick, wooly gloves, very thick, wooly gloves. Another kept telling herself that her hands were getting warmer, warmer, warmer.

They were, too. Slowly, the needles on the temperature trainers began to move. The Greens' subjects saw the movement and realized that they were doing something right. They redoubled their efforts—and the needles responded by rising still farther. The biofeedback they were getting offered both information and reward. With its help, ordinary Americans were duplicating one of the "tricks" of the Eastern mystics. They were producing an above-normal temperature in one part of the body while maintaining a normal temperature overall.

However, not all of the Greens' subjects were equally successful at warming their hands. One woman in particular was having a difficult time. Eventually, she spoke to a researcher. She could feel a headache coming on, she said, one of her excruciatingly painful migraines. Could she just forget about the experiment for the time being and relax? When she felt well enough, she would go home and go to bed.

No problem, the researcher responded. The woman should just sit back and not worry about a thing.

The researcher was pleasant but busy. Too busy to remember to disconnect the woman from the temperature trainer. And the woman was too distraught to think to ask to be disconnected.

That is how the Greens discovered biofeedback as a treatment for migraine. Without really being aware she was doing it, the woman went on staring at the temperature meter. As the needle continued to rise, she continued to try, half unconsciously, to raise it farther. She succeeded, *and as she did, her headache began to go away.*

Intrigued by the results of this accidental experiment, the Greens began investigating the link between hand

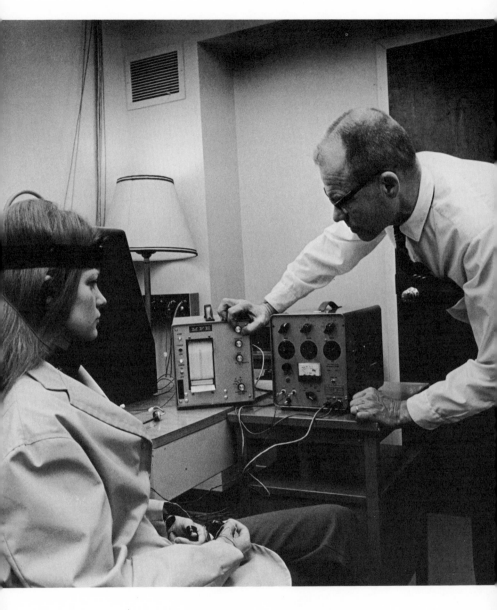

Dr. Elmer Green works with a subject
at the Menninger Foundation.

Alyce Green is training a young woman to control her migraine headaches.

temperature and migraine. Their conclusion, and the conclusion of other doctors as well, is that migraines are related to the flow of blood through the forehead. Blood flow there seems to increase during a migraine attack. As the attack abates, blood flow decreases. Unlike a tension headache, a migraine is apparently not caused by the tightening of muscles in the forehead and neck.

This would explain why hand warming helped the woman's headache. Warming her hands meant increasing blood flow to them. The increase was accomplished when blood vessels in her hands dilated—opened wider. After dilation, blood rushed in more quickly. At the same time, apparently, blood vessels in the woman's forehead and temples constricted—got narrower. Blood flow slowed there. Result: No more migraine.

The Greens, and other biofeedback researchers, too, claim to have had much success in treating migraine. One of the Greens' patients, a Kansas woman named Lillian Petroni, described her headaches before treatment. "I had spots in front of my eyes, terrible nausea, and a pounding headache over one eye . . . I simply couldn't stay on my feet. I couldn't tolerate light . . . I couldn't tolerate noise . . . I could not talk to people. I was just in constant, agonizing pain."

Mrs. Petroni had a five-year history of migraine when she went to Elmer and Alyce Green. After a mere two weeks of biofeedback training, she had "learned" to "shut off" a headache at the first sign of pain. A three-year followup showed that her migraines had not returned.

Being able to control blood flow through the body seems an amazing skill. But it was only one of the amazing skills people were learning through biofeedback as the 1970s began.

Among the most impressive stories of biofeedback

research was one that came out of the Canadian laboratory of Dr. John Basmajian. Working at the Chedoke Medical Center in Hamilton, Ontario, Basmajian set out to demonstrate that a person could be trained to control tiny muscle movements using just a single nerve cell at a time.

The human body contains about a quarter of a million individual "motor neurons." These are nerve cells located in the spinal column that allow voluntary muscle movements to occur.

Suppose you want to reach out to turn the page of this book. The message—*Reach Out, Hand*—travels from your brain to those nerve cells in your spine that activate and control your hand movements. The appropriate nerve cells fire, and your hand muscles contract, allowing you to make the precise movement you want.

Ordinarily, nerve cells fire in groups, at the rate of about twenty times per second. That is because a single nerve cell may control only three or four muscle cells. Three or four cells are not nearly enough to produce significant movement in a hand. Many times that number of nerve cells must fire if you are going to lift your arm and extend your hand. They—and other groups of nerve cells that control wrist, hand, and finger movements—must fire repeatedly until you have finished turning the page.

Basmajian recruited a group of volunteers who were willing to try to learn to control their nerve cells on a one-by-one basis. He inserted electrodes into certain of their muscle cell groups. The electrodes were linked to biofeedback equipment—recording devices and loudspeakers.

As we have seen, muscle cells give off minute electrical charges when they move. The electrodes picked up these charges. The loudspeakers amplified them into short, sharp sounds.

At first the sounds came loud and fast, as large numbers of nerve cells fired in unison. Guided by what they were hearing, the volunteers concentrated on producing just one note at a time. Soon they were doing exactly that. Their brains were telling their nerve cells to fire independently, and the nerve cells obeyed.

As Basmajian's subjects grew more and more adept at working their motor neurons, strange, haunting rhythms filled the lab. The volunteers had learned to "play" their nerve cells like musical instruments!

Much more than music was involved in Basmajian's experiment, however. He had demonstrated that people can learn to exercise exquisitely fine control over parts of their bodies. This demonstration helped to usher in a new age of biofeedback medicine. From around the country came report after report of seemingly miraculous cures.

At Emory University Medical Center in Atlanta, Georgia, for example, doctors were working with an 18-year-old brain-damaged girl. The damage had occurred eight years earlier, the result of an auto accident. It affected the nerves and muscles that controlled the girl's leg movements. Every time she tried to place her heel on the ground—as one normally does in walking—the muscles of her calves clenched in a paralyzing spasm. Surgery to lengthen the tendons in the girl's heels seemed to be her only hope.

Then someone suggested trying biofeedback. Electrodes were attached to the girl's calf muscles and to an electromyograph. Each time she started to take a step, the muscles began a spasm. That set off a buzzer. To stop the buzzer, the girl had to stop the spasm.

The girl concentrated, just as Basmajian's volunteers had concentrated on producing individual notes over the loudspeakers. Bit by bit, she developed a technique for silencing the buzzer. At the end of three training sessions, the girl was walking normally.

In much the same way, biofeedback has been used with children whose brains have been damaged by the condition known as cerebral palsy (CP). CP children frequently experience muscle spasms. Their limbs and bodies move jerkily, awkwardly. Some find it impossible to walk, to dress, or to feed themselves.

At Children's Hospital in Boston, Massachusetts, children with CP have been linked to biofeedback equipment and instructed to practice a specific movement. When the movement is performed correctly, the child is rewarded with a musical tune. The tune lasts until the child's muscles begin a new series of spasms. The child works to keep the music going as long as possible, to keep movement flowing smoothly.

The paralyzed, or partially paralyzed, can also be helped by biofeedback. Biofeedback allows patients to "watch" or "listen to" the faint electrical signals from damaged limbs. Those signals, isolated and amplified, let patients know exactly what they are doing to produce tiny movements in those limbs. They help patients learn to make those movements more and more similar to normal movements. Eventually, such people, like the woman with the facial tic whom we saw in Chapter 1, may regain full or partial movement.

Biofeedback has also helped people whose movement disorders have a different cause. One dramatic case involved a man whose spine had been damaged by a gunshot wound. Three years later, the man was still struggling, unsuccessfully, to learn to walk with crutches and braces. His problem: Every time he stood upright, his blood pressure plunged. Every time, he fainted.

But the man was persistent. He entered an experimental biofeedback training program and concentrated on learning to raise his blood pressure. Within a short time, he

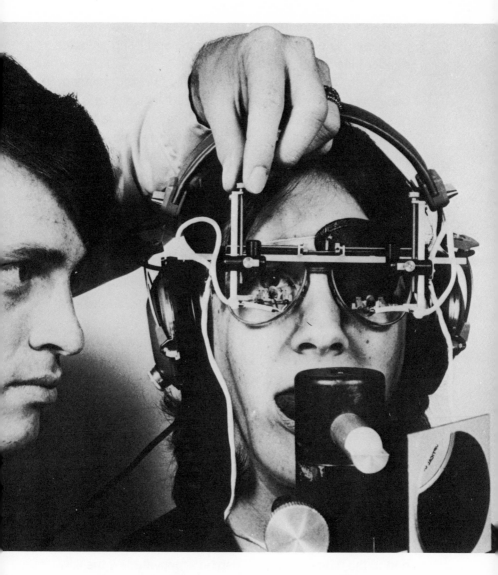

In an interesting application of biofeedback to treat movement disorders, a researcher uses an elaborate sound apparatus to help a patient control a wandering or "lazy" eye.

was able to stand without fainting. Soon he was walking. Four years later, he was still walking—and living an independent life in his own home.

Even for those who are permanently crippled, biofeedback has its uses. Some motorized wheelchairs are designed to be operated through minute muscle movements or through a system of controlled eye movements. Biofeedback training can enable the crippled to refine such movements with precision.

Victims of stroke are other candidates for biofeedback training. Some people who have had strokes lose the sense of where their arms and legs are in space. This condition, called proprioception, makes normal movement— walking, sitting, standing—nearly impossible. In one study, almost 70 percent of a group of men and women with proprioception showed improvement after five weeks of biofeedback training sessions.

Besides being used to help alleviate various physical handicaps, biofeedback, according to adherents, can play a role in preventive medicine. People who use it to learn to lower their blood pressure, for example, may be helping to prevent serious illnesses, such as heart attack or stroke, at a later date. Other patients have been trained—like the rats in Dr. Neal Miller's curare experiments—to alter their heartbeat rate. Such an ability could be useful in correcting what might be life-threatening irregularities in the heartbeat.

Ulcers may also be preventable through biofeedback. An ulcer is a painful "sore" in the stomach or in another part of the digestive tract. It can be aggravated by the flow of gastric juices, the highly acid substances that aid digestion.

Can biofeedback teach people with ulcers, or people

considered likely to get ulcers, to reduce their flow of gastric juices? Some scientists think it is possible.

A few scientists are even convinced that people can learn to use biofeedback-like techniques to cure themselves of cancer. At the Cancer Counseling and Research Center in Fort Worth, Texas, Dr. Carl Simonton has employed "mental imaging" to help cancer patients fight their disease. Dr. Simonton told his patients to imagine that their tumors were hunks of raw meat. They visualized this "meat" being attacked and devoured by schools of hungry fish. The "fish" were their own white blood cells, part of the body's disease defense system. Over a four-year period, Dr. Simonton worked with 159 patients, none of whom was expected to live more than a year. Of those patients, 63 were still alive when the study ended. Their average survival time: Over *two* years. The average survival rate of those patients who died was more than twenty months, eight months longer than predicted.

Other doctors think it may one day be possible to use biofeedback to teach cancer patients to "starve" their tumors. Just as migraine victims learn to decrease the flow of blood to their foreheads, the doctors say, people with cancer might learn to "direct" their bloodstreams to stop carrying nourishment to malignant growths.

Doctors are treating other conditions through biofeedback. At New York City's Columbia Presbyterian Medical Center, twenty-two men and women with severe blood clots were given training. The clots were cutting off circulation through their legs, and the patients could not walk two city blocks without experiencing intense pain. During biofeedback training, they were taught to raise the temperature of their legs. That meant dilating their blood vessels and sending more blood there. Five months later, all twenty-two patients could walk as much as a mile—without pain.

Another startling medical use of biofeedback involves tinnitus. "Tinnitus" comes from the Latin word that means "to jingle," and people with this condition are plagued by continual whistling, ringing, and pounding noises in the ears. This makes it difficult for them to hear outside sounds, such as music or conversation.

At the University of Buffalo, Dr. Sanford Hoffman used biofeedback with a group of tinnitus patients who ranged in age from 27 to 70. Each patient was linked to an EMG, which amplified electrical activity in the muscles of the forehead. By learning to relax those muscles, 60 percent of Dr. Hoffman's patients reported a hearing improvement.

Even the profoundly deaf have been helped through biofeedback. At the University of Alabama Medical Center in Birmingham, researchers are using a "palatometer" to teach deaf children to speak. The palatometer uses visual feedback. It shows children how their tongues are moving as they try to pronounce words aloud. At the same time, it shows them how a hearing person's tongue moves when he or she pronounces the same words. By comparing the two, the deaf can learn to communicate more clearly.

Learning *not* to speak is the point of another area of biofeedback medicine. In this case, the patients are people who subvocalize as they read to themselves. Subvocalizing means mouthing the words silently while reading—a habit that slows a reader down and produces tiredness as well. Schoolteachers know that many of their poor readers suffer from a tendency to subvocalize.

In biofeedback training to overcome subvocalization, electrodes are placed on the neck. These electrodes detect tiny movements of the vocal muscles and transmit them to an EMG, where they are amplified as sound. The more muscle movement, the louder the sound. The subvocalizer strives to keep the sound as low as possible. Eventually, subvocalization may stop, and reading skills improve.

Stutterers have been helped by similar techniques. Here, too, the equipment picks up and amplifies unnecessary muscle contractions, contractions that cause the stuttering. Gradually, the stutterer learns better control of the muscles.

Learning to control pain is another biofeedback possibility. We've already seen how biofeedback has helped people who suffer from headaches, both migraines and those caused by tension. In Portland, Maine, Dr. JoAnn Miller uses biofeedback and other techniques to help both arthritic patients and those with bone injuries. Some patients have cut in half the amount of pain-killing drugs they take after just a few weeks of therapy, she claims. In Denver, Colorado, Dr. Ed Gilbert of Presbyterian Medical Center has found biofeedback helpful in relieving the pain of cancer victims.

Biofeedback to reduce pain, to cure cancer, to prevent disease—these are only a few of the uses that biofeedback enthusiasts envision for the method. But perhaps even more impressive than what biofeedback accomplishes, these enthusiasts say, is *how* it accomplishes what it does. Biofeedback works as medicine by involving patients—mind and body—in their own therapies. Biofeedback's greatest value, they believe, is that it allows people to take responsibility for controlling their own health. And that, they add, goes for mental health, too.

MAKING WAVES WITH ALPHA

Of all possible uses for biofeedback, perhaps the one that excites the greatest enthusiasm among researchers is the one that has to do with alpha. As we saw in Chapter 1, "alpha" is the name given to a particular type of human brain-wave pattern.

The name was chosen back in the 1920s by a German scientist, Hans Berger. Berger was convinced that the brain gives off electrical energy. Furthermore, he contended that the way this energy is given off can vary from time to time. Those variations are related to different human feelings—happiness, tension, anxiety, relaxation, and so forth.

Although he found little support for such theories among other scientists, Berger plunged ahead with his research. During the summer of 1924 he began working with a mentally disturbed teenager. Berger placed two electrodes on the patient's head. The electrodes were connected to a galvanometer. The galvanometer, an early device for measuring and recording electrical output, was named after Luigi Galvani, an eighteenth-century Italian scientist. Galvani was one of the first to speculate about the nature of electricity.

As Berger watched the galvanometer, it began record-ing an electrical charge. His patient was indeed emitting electrical brain waves.

Berger continued this line of research for another five years. At the end of that time he announced that he had discovered and defined two entirely separate types of brain waves. The first, as recorded on the galvanometer, produced a rhythmic, wavelike pattern. In general, it appeared when the person was in a relaxed state of mind. Berger labeled this pattern alpha. Alpha is the first letter in the Greek alphabet.

The second brain-wave pattern appeared as smaller and tighter than the first. Peaks and valleys were closer together and much less pronounced. It seemed to be pres-ent when the patient was concentrating or trying to solve a problem. Berger named this pattern after the second Greek letter, beta.

Since Berger's time, scientists have discovered two additional kinds of brain waves—theta and delta. Delta is a sleep pattern. Theta appears to be associated with both creativity and anxiety.

Thirty years after Berger's experiments, American scientists began to be intrigued by the possibility of a link between brain activity and mood. To scientists working with biofeedback, the idea had a special attraction. Sup-pose, through biofeedback, people could be trained to increase their production of relaxing alpha waves. They would have an ever-present, drug-free shortcut to restful-ness and peace of mind.

Dr. Barbara Brown of the Sepulveda, California, Veter-ans' Administration Hospital and Dr. Joe Kamiya of the University of Chicago and later of the Langely Porter Neu-ropsychiatric Institute in San Francisco decided to follow up on this idea. Kamiya published his results in 1969; Brown, a year later.

Both used more sophisticated equipment than had been available to Berger. Their basic tool was the electroencephalograph (EEG)—consisting of electrodes, an amplifier, and a recording mechanism. The electrodes, which are attached to the scalp, pick up electrical signals from the brain. These are amplified. The amplified signals activate a row of pens that rest lightly against a sheet of paper. As the paper is rolled by, the pens record the signal pattern. The sharp, close peaks and valleys of a beta pattern, the more open alpha pattern, theta and delta patterns—all are easily distinguishable on the EEG.

Researchers watched the EEG patterns and used them to provide biofeedback for their subjects. In Kamiya's lab, that feedback came in the form of a musical tone. When the subjects could hear the tone, they knew they were emitting alpha.

Knowing that, the patients were able to isolate those thoughts and feelings that produced the alpha pattern. Soon they were producing more and more alpha. "Just as rats can be taught to press a bar," Kamiya reported, "so people can be taught conscious control of their brain activity in a relatively short time."

In Dr. Brown's lab, the procedure was somewhat different. Alpha signals from her subjects were treated electronically to produce a steady flow of current. The current powered a blue light. The more alpha, the bluer the color appeared. If there was no alpha, the light went out.

Brown's subjects concentrated on keeping the light as blue as possible. Her report: "By the end of the first practice session [90 minutes, including several 3-minute rest periods], the average subject had more than doubled the amount of alpha in his EEG, and he tripled the amount during the third practice session."

But would Brown's subjects be able to produce alpha waves at will outside the lab? Unless they could, learning the technique would do them little good. A further problem was that in the course of their hectic daily lives the subjects might think they were producing alpha when they really were not. Experiments have shown that this can happen. Or, as Dr. Brown put it: "It occurred to me that if the experimental subjects had truly learned to control their own alpha, then they should be able to perform the feat *without* the help of bio-feedback."

A new series of experiments showed that the subjects could do just that. A month after the original work, the same subjects were asked to return to the lab to try to produce alpha waves without the help of biofeedback. (They were still attached to the EEGs, but only the researchers could see the patterns produced by the moving pens. There were no blue lights.)

The subjects were instructed to turn on switches whenever they thought they were producing alpha. When they did not think they were producing alpha, they were to turn off the switches. "Over an hour's recording time, the accuracy of the subjects for knowing when alpha was present ranged between 75 and 100 percent," Brown wrote. "Even two months later, accuracy remained above 70 percent."

With such accuracy, people would be powerfully equipped to use alpha in their everyday lives. They might use it, for instance, to combat anxiety.

The term "anxiety" covers a range of emotions. It can be mild—"I probably should study harder for this test," or "Can I earn enough this summer to buy a good second-hand car?"—or it can be severe. A person suffering from a severe anxiety attack may feel faint or nauseous. The victim may experience a wildly pounding heart, shortness of breath, or other physical symptoms.

The way to deal with such symptoms could be to learn to increase alpha output—to enter an alpha state. In 1978 Dr. Joe Kamiya and an associate, Dr. James V. Hardt, published a study showing that alpha feedback training may be useful in relieving anxiety.

To begin the study, the two researchers selected a sample of 100 college men. First the men were given a personality test designed to measure feelings of anxiety. Of the 100 men who took the test, the 8 indicated by the test as most anxious and the 8 indicated as the least anxious were chosen to continue.

The 16 young men were put through a seven-day alpha biofeedback training course. They learned both to *increase* alpha production and to *decrease* it. The low-anxiety group was highly successful at learning to alter alpha output in both directions. However, Dr. Kamiya found that the alterations did not affect anxiety levels in this group very much. That is, the men who were not particularly anxious to begin with did not get much more anxious when they decreased alpha. Nor did they become much less anxious when they increased it.

For the highly anxious group, the results were different. The people in this group were less adept than the others at altering alpha output. But when they did alter it, the effects were greater than those in the first group. Suppressing alpha meant an increase in anxiety for these men, and increasing alpha meant less anxiety. From this study, Kamiya and Hardt concluded that "long-term alpha feedback training (at least five hours) may be useful in anxiety therapy."

It may be useful in other therapies as well. Several mild mental disorders might be relieved through alpha training.

tern that can be conveyed via feedback to the individual who generated it.'' The individual could then learn to reproduce that pattern whenever he or she needs it.

There is another reason for the enthusiasm many people feel for biofeedback. Through it, Western society and Western science have discovered a way to consider and to evaluate the physical and mental achivements of Eastern mysticism.

Not long ago, the West dismissed those accomplishments out of hand. ''Knowing'' as they did that mind and body are completely separate and that mental processes cannot affect autonomic systems, most Westerners had no doubt that yogis and others were simply clever tricksters.

Biofeedback has helped to modify that attitude. Western scientists, using Western methods and safeguards against cheating, have checked the performances of various yogis. Several of the tests have verified the mystics' claims.

In one test, conducted at the All-India Institute of Medical Science in New Delhi, a yogi named Ramanand was locked into an air-tight box. Inside the box was just enough air to last for ninety minutes. Left in the box longer than that, a person would suffocate—unless that person could slow his breathing to an exceedingly low rate. That is what Yogi Ramanand said he could do. And he did. Only after a full six hours in the box did Ramanand press the emergency buzzer that notified the scientists that he wanted to be released.

Dr. Elmer Green and others worked with a yogi at the Menninger Foundation, too. Carefully monitored by up-to-date equipment, the yogi speeded up his heartbeat rate to five times greater than normal. None of the scientists present could detect any movement of his skeletal muscles or

For many years western scientists refused to believe
yogis could control their physical state in ways
that would allow them to perform such feats as
sitting on a couch of nails, lowering their
body temperatures, or reducing their heartbeats.

any change in his breathing. In other words, the yogi was changing his heart rate solely through the power of his mind.

Similarly, the yogi proved his claim that he could produce a ten-degree temperature difference between the thumb and little finger of the same hand. As Dr. Green and others watched, one side of the Indian's hand grew hot and flushed. The other side turned cool and gray.

Going into a deep trance is another feat that Eastern mystics including yogis and Japanese Zen masters, claim the ability to do. Again, Western science has validated at least some of the claims. A remarkable demonstration took place in a remote cave on the Ganges River high in the Himalayas of India. There, an elderly yogi was linked to an EEG. Electrodes were placed on his palms and over his heart. The yogi put himself into a trance.

All the machines agreed: The yogi's trance was absolute. He was not distracted by sudden movement or noise; neither his skin, nor his heart, nor his brain gave any indication that he was remotely aware of the activity produced by the scientists.

Interestingly enough, the EEG showed that the yogi was in a deeply relaxing alpha state throughout his trance. The evidence seemed conclusive. Mind and body could no longer be considered separately. They belong together. They work together to regulate thousands of systems, voluntary and involuntary, throughout the body. Together, they govern physical and mental health. Together they offer patients and doctors potent new tools for maintaining good health and curing illness. Beyond that, brain-wave therapy suggests exciting pathways toward working with the subconscious and toward expanding the human mind in new ways and new directions.

It was the early 1970s. Enthusiasm for biofeedback had reached greater heights than ever before.

Then came shocking news. Dr. Neal Miller had repudiated the curare experiments he had carried out on rats over a decade earlier. "It is prudent not to rely on any of the experiments on curarized animals for evidence," he wrote in 1978.

Unexpectedly, biofeedback had had one of its important theoretical props knocked clean out from under it.

5

FAILURES, DOUBTS, AND QUESTIONS

Why did Dr. Miller disavow his curare experiments? Those experiments seemed to have proved that animals can be taught, by operant conditioning, to control at least some of their involuntary functions. That control, according to the evidence of Miller's work does not depend upon use of the skeletal muscles and the central nervous system.

As we saw in Chapter 2, Miller's first successful curare experiment involved "teaching" rats to speed up and to slow down their heartbeat rates. After that, Miller and his associates carried out similar trials. Their results appeared to verify the first findings. Some of these later experiments were conducted under Miller's supervision; some, under the supervision of other scientists at Rockefeller University. In addition, the results were confirmed by scientists at two other laboratories. Scientists call such independent confirmation "replication."

Replication is an important principle in scientific research. It means doing an experiment over and over again, using the same procedures, and *always getting the same result*. Unless an experiment can be replicated by a number of different scientists, the scientific community in general will not accept it. Relying upon replication is a way

of guarding against errors resulting from careless lab procedures. It is also a guard against outright cheating by scientists more eager to build their reputations than to carry out honest research.

Although replication was not a problem for the Miller curare experiments at first, it soon became one. During the 1970s, several scientists tried to reproduce the original results. All failed. So, now, did Miller.

What had gone wrong? Rather bitterly, Miller suggested that perhaps he and his assistants had been victims of a "mass hallucination" when they observed the first successful experiments. Of course, he was not serious. A hallucination at Rockefeller University in 1966 would hardly account for the fact that there *was* replication in other parts of the country two or three years later. More seriously, Miller suggested that the form of curare he used, *d*-tubocurarine, could have changed between the late 1960s and the early 1970s.

Miller and an associate, Barry Dworkin, decided to look into this idea. To begin with, executives at the company that had manufactured the *d*-tubocurarine assured the scientists that no such change was possible. But further investigation by Miller and Dworkin revealed that *d*-tubocurarine is refined from a substance found in the vine of a South American plant called *Strychnos toxifera*. That substance might vary slightly in quality from plant to plant. In that case, the quality of the refined product would vary, too. Miller and Dworkin reasoned that there might have

Dr. Neal Miller in his laboratory
at Rockefeller University in 1978.

been impurities in the d-tubocurarine of the 1960s but not in that of the 1970s. Those impurities could have affected their experimental results.

Another possibility Miller suggested was that there might have been changes in the rats he and others used. Several companies are in the business of breeding and raising animals for sale to schools and laboratories.

At times, people at such companies change the way they produce the animals. For example, they may make conditions more sterile or find ways to reduce stress in the animals. Changes like these might well have resulted in animals that were slightly different in the 1970s from those of the 1960s. With different animals, the results of the experiments would have been different too.

Looking at his own lab, Miller came up with another idea. The respiratory equipment used in the earlier experiments—the device that enabled the paralyzed rats to breathe—was relatively crude. Perhaps its workings had confused the results.

That was possible, of course. It was also possible that the rats had changed their characteristics over the years or that the d-tubocurarine become purer, or less pure, as time went by. But some other scientists were skeptical of such suggestions. They pointed out that Miller's ideas focused on mechanical and procedural problems. That was wrong, they thought. In their view, the failure to replicate had more to do with Miller's basic assumptions regarding how animals learn.

Granted, these scientists said, Miller's rats had not used their skeletal muscles in any clear-cut or measurable way. But giving the rats curare did not prevent their brains from firing signals to those muscles. Perhaps, in the words of one scientist, each rat was using the skeletal muscles "in its head." In that case, the central nervous system would have been involved. Thus, a number of scientists concluded, the curare experiments did not show positively that Miller's ideas were correct. They did not absolutely rule out the possibility that the central nervous system and the skeletal muscles must somehow be involved in any learning through operant conditioning. Even Dr. Miller agreed that this possibility must be considered.

The failure to replicate the Miller experiments left biofeedback in an odd position. On the one hand, researchers in the field could no longer point to the work of one of this country's leading psychologists as proof that living creatures can assume voluntary control of autonomic functions. On the other hand, their own research was showing that people *were* controlling such functions and, in the process, getting rid of migraines and hypertension, moving once-paralyzed limbs, curing stuttering—possibly even making inroads against cancers.

"Perhaps the most remarkable aspect of the curare experience," wrote Dr. L. E. Roberts in 1978, "is . . . that the enthusiasm generated by these studies carried them into the published literature and raised strong expectations of success before subsequent efforts . . . revealed the tenuous and misleading nature of the original findings." He meant that while people in biofeedback were plunging ahead with research into such arcane matters as brain-wave manipulation and cancer cures, they were ignoring some basic issues.

Very basic issues. Some critics of biofeedback techniques think that researchers ought to begin by investigating how biofeedback works. Others think they might start by finding out *whether* it works.

How can anyone doubt that it does? Look at the men and women who have been cured of excruciating headaches. Certainly their experiences were real. They suffered terrible pain. They went through biofeedback training to learn techniques that somehow eliminated that pain. They were cured.

Actually, the story is not that simple, the critics say. It leaves out several factors, among them, the placebo effect.

A placebo is something—a drug, a device, a therapy—that appears to be effective but really is not. Scientists often use placebos to test new medicines. Suppose, for instance, they are trying out a new pain reliever on a group of volunteers. The volunteers, all of whom have headaches, are divided into two groups. To the men and women in the first group, the scientists give a dose of the new drug. To those in the second group, they give a dose that looks exactly like the drug. It smells and tastes the same, too. In fact, the people who take it believe that it is the same drug.

In reality, however, it is a harmless sugar pill, one that can have no medicinal effect upon the pain of a headache. But since the people who take it do not know that, some may find that their headaches disappear anyway. That is what is known as the placebo effect. Believing that they are swallowing an effective new medicine makes them feel better.

Similarly, some people in the first group—the group that really did get the medicine—will also feel better simply because they think they ought to. For others, though, the pills will be genuinely effective, and their headaches will improve—assuming that the new medicine does have pain-killing qualities. If there are many cures in the first group, and only a small number in the second, scientists will conclude that the new pill does indeed work.

This sort of experiment allows scientists to separate the placebo effect from the effect of the actual treatment.

Tests with placebos are an essential part of evaluating any new medical technique.

Placebo tests have been part of the evaluation of biofeedback, too. In general, though, they have been an unsuccessful part.

Biofeedback researchers find it difficult to design placebo experiments. Picture the problem. A researcher divides her volunteers into two groups. People in both groups are told that they are going to learn to decrease heartbeat rate. They are conducted to the lab and wired to EEG machines and biofeedback equipment. The experiment begins.

For the group getting correct feedback signals, everything goes smoothly. For the other group, there is trouble. The people in this group are getting false feedback. Every time their heartbeats come a little farther apart, they are told that they are coming closer together. They are doing everything all wrong, the signals say.

Many of the people may know better. It's not hard to tell whether your heart is beating more and more slowly—or faster and faster. Some volunteers who are getting false feedback may ignore it. Others may get angry and pull out of the experiment.

In one instance, a man was supposed to be learning to overcome a stutter. He was told that he needed to relax the muscles of his larynx. The man tried to do so.

What this man did not know was that he was part of an experiment on the placebo effect. As he tried to relax, feedback from another patient was substituted for what he should have been getting. The more he relaxed, the more negative feedback he got. Before long, the man called the researchers into the room—to tell them that their machinery had broken down!

Responsible biofeedback researchers know how important it is to their science to find reliable ways of testing for the placebo effect. As Neal Miller points out, "Placebo effects are particularly prominent with some of the symptoms that have been involved in biofeedback treatment." Headaches, he adds, respond "flagrantly" to placebos.

A second factor that confuses evaluation of biofeedback techniques is that of the patient–therapist relationship. This is closely related to the placebo effect.

Everyone has heard of doctors with a good "bedside manner." These are the doctors who seem to cure by their very personalities—warm, encouraging, caring. Patients feel better just talking to such doctors. They are eager to follow the physicians' recommendations, and such positive attitudes can do much to bring about a quick recovery. Is it the same with biofeedback? Can the therapist's manner affect a subject's response?

During the 1970s, a scientist named Edward Taub began a series of experiments aimed at teaching people to control skin temperature with the help of biofeedback training. With several assistants, Taub got to work in his Silver Spring, Maryland, laboratory.

One assistant was exceptionally enthusiastic about the experiments. Her assignment was to train twenty-one subjects in the skin-warming technique. She devoted herself to the job with zest. Another assistant, delegated to work with twenty-two subjects, was skeptical about the experi-

One criticism of biofeedback techniques is that the relationship between therapist and subject influences the outcome of the training session.

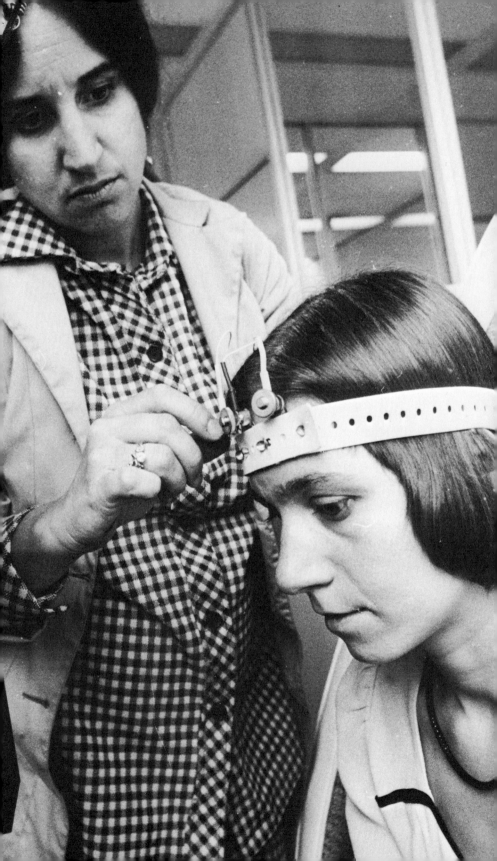

ment. She maintained a carefully neutral attitude as she went about her work.

The results of Taub's experiment left no doubt about the importance of the therapist's attitude in biofeedback training. Nineteen of the enthusiastic assistant's subjects learned to change skin temperature. Only two of the other assistant's subjects learned to do the same thing. Although Taub did not set out to demonstrate the influence of patient–therapist relationships, he definitely succeeded in doing so.

Yet Taub's work raises more questions than it answers. The relationship between subject and trainer is important in biofeedback—but how important? Can biofeedback training succeed without an enthusiastic trainer? And if enthusiasm is essential, how important is the feedback itself? Would just talking to a helpful therapist or doctor do as much for a patient as being wired up to all that machinery?

Many critics of biofeedback are convinced that it would. They remind us that up to 75 percent of illness may be caused by stress and tension. Take a person suffering from a stress-related condition and talk to him warmly and sympathetically. Let him rest in a quiet room for several hours each week. Encourage him. Tell him he's performing well. After that, the only surprise would be if he did not begin to feel better.

Biofeedback researchers have published thousands of reports on their findings. Even so, hard, provable facts about biofeedback's effectiveness are difficult to come by. That's a third area of perplexity for people trying to evaluate the technique.

Part of this problem involves the fact that biofeedback hasn't yet been investigated over a very long period of time. Many studies last only a few weeks. Sometimes there is no follow-up. Even when there is, that follow-up may come too soon after the original work was done. Barbara Brown followed up on her alpha-training experiment by checking to see how well her subjects had retained their new skill. But her follow-up came only two months after the training. A two-month period is not long enough to validate a medical therapy. Drugs, for instance, may be tested for ten or more years before they are used in actual practice.

Another part of the problem has to do with the size of the experimental samples. Most studies have involved only small numbers of people. In Fort Worth, Dr. Carl Simonton worked with 159 cancer patients. He reported encouraging results, but the experiences of 159 people are not enough from which to draw many meaningful conclusions. In Buffalo, Dr. Sanford Hoffman reported that two-thirds of a group of tinnitus patients said that their condition was helped through biofeedback training. But the group only numbered 18. Dr. Hoffman was reporting positive findings based on information from just a dozen people.

Furthermore it is necessary to ask how valid that information is. According to Hoffman, the 12 patients either reported decreased noise levels or said that the noise they heard no longer bothered them as much. What does that mean, "No longer bothered them as much"? That the noise remained the same—or even got worse—but that they had learned to live with it? That the therapists were friendly and helpful and made the patients feel better about their hearing difficulties? That they simply enjoyed the contact with Dr. Hoffman and his staff?

A personal, subjective report, such as "it doesn't bother me as much," tells a scientist little about a patient's condition. Yet biofeedback researchers must frequently rely on such reports. They are the only means of describing changes in a headache or in a mood, for example. Only when researchers are working with something that can be measured, such as blood pressure or heartbeat rate, can they feel reasonably sure that they have hard, objective evidence about the results of a particular biofeedback technique.

Yet even such objective evidence may not be completely reliable. Some patients have shown a measurably lower blood pressure after taking a sugar pill. What's more, a biofeedback technique that can be proved to have worked for Patient A in November may not work for Patient B that same month. It may not work for Patient A the following March, either. The reason: The "variables" are so great.

A psychologist at the University of Houston, Gordon Paul, has drawn up a schedule of variables with which bio-feedback researchers must contend. To begin, there are variables in patients. These fall into three categories. There are variations in the nature of their physical and mental conditions; in their personal and social characteristics; and in their everyday environments. One migraine sufferer may have frequent painful headaches, be a wealthy but lonely widow, have lots of free time, and rely heavily upon tranquilizers and alcohol. Another may have occasional headaches, be a factory worker with eight children, and never touch drugs. A third may have two or three migraines a year, be a twice-married suburban math teacher, and so on. The patient variables are endless.

Then there are the therapist variables. Dr. Paul also categorizes these into three classes: differences in methods and techniques; in personal and social characteristics; and in characteristics of the treatment setting (whether it is a hospital or a clinic, low cost or expensive, and so forth). A third group of variables concerns time: how long treatment lasts, whether or not there is follow-up, and other factors.

Summing it up, Dr. Paul remarks that the question about biofeedback should be not "Does it work?" but, rather, "*What* treatment, by *whom,* is most effective for *this* individual with *that* specific problem, and under *which* set of circumstances?" It will be a laborious process to discover objective criteria by which to scientifically evaluate such complexity.

Variables are something that biofeedback patients and therapists bring into the lab with them. They are something the patients go back to when treatment is over, as well. That brings up another area of criticism. Many doctors and scientists contend that successful biofeedback training in the lab or clinic may not carry over into the "real world" outside.

Take the case of the second patient we met in Chapter 1, the young woman who had had a brain hemorrhage. Biofeedback training in the hospital enabled her to lower her blood pressure dramatically. When she left the hospital, though, she became aware of the problems she would face. She was partly paralyzed. She realized how much trouble she would have getting around the city. Living alone would be tough. She needed an operation on one eye. When would she be fit to return to work? The worries mounted—and so did her blood pressure. After returning from her Caribbean vacation, the patient began a new series of training sessions, but they were unsuccessful. What had worked once, in a hospital, did not work again when the patient was at home. This, unfortunately, has been the experience of many biofeedback patients.

Other problems can arise when biofeedback leaves the

lab. Oddly enough, some patients actually need their ill-nesses. If biofeedback brings about a cure, the patient can suffer.

One such case occurred at the Menninger Foundation. A woman came to Dr. Green to learn to control her migraines. Therapy seemed to be succeeding. Then, just as the woman was becoming able to "turn off" a head-ache, she lost the skill. The migraines returned.

Dr. Green was puzzled, but eventually the woman her-self realized what was going on. She needed her illness. Her husband was in the habit of bringing home company for dinner and on weekends, and the woman hated that. Her defense—her way of getting out of having to cook, clean, and entertain—was to develop a headache.

This patient was lucky. Recognizing her problem, she could deal with it. She could decide to go on having the headaches, or she could confront her husband and demand that he stop bringing so many people home.

On the other hand, the dilemma may not be so simple. What if the husband refuses to change his ways? The wife may have to choose between migraines and a divorce. What about a patient with, for example, ulcers? If biofeed-back training helps him to relieve that condition, will he develop another, even more serious, illness? It could hap-pen, critics warn. Barbara Brown even wonders what might happen if mentally unstable persons learn a skill like that of altering heartbeat rate. Some might use it as a means of inducing heart attacks, thereby committing sui-cide, she fears.

Another warning concerns the expertise and qualifica-tions of people who operate biofeedback clinics. This warning comes from many who are enthusiastic about bio-feedback, as well as from critics outside the field. Some people who claim to be experts in biofeedback techniques may not really know what they are doing. Their equipment may be faulty. They may be training unsuspecting men and women to alter their vital functions in harmful ways.

For example, some researchers believe that people who suffer from epilepsy may be able to use biofeedback to learn to ward off a seizure. Epilepsy is thought to be caused by electrical irregularities within the brain. Using biofeedback to control those irregularities would be a drugless way of mastering the disease. But an ignorant therapist might train an epileptic incorrectly. Instead of learning to avoid attacks, the patient might be taught to produce effects that could bring them on.

A similar danger is that people may try to use biofeedback on their own, without training from any therapist whatsoever. Already this is possible. Various kinds of biofeedback equipment—EEG-like machines, alpha detectors, "muscle monitors," "electronic aspirin," even devices designed to be used with a home computer—are offered for sale through mail-order advertisements in newspapers, magazines, and catalogues.

Reputable biofeedback researchers utter strict warnings about self-treatment with such machines. Buying them could be a simple waste of money. One Massachusetts biofeedback researcher points out that there is "a huge 'sucker' market for the kinds of gear that are supposed to permit easy recording of bioelectric signals." The machines may not work as they are supposed to.

Worse dangers may confront those who try biofeedback self-treatment. It could, in the words of Barbara Brown, "result in the inadvertent training of people to aggravate or even incite actual illness." Dr. Brown also thinks that the result of self-treatment could be to mask the symptoms of serious illness. A person who has real heart problems might be slow to recognize that fact if she has learned to alter her heart rhythms. A person who thinks he is suffering from tension headaches, and who turns to biofeedback to learn to relax neck and forehead muscles, may really have a brain tumor.

Misuse of alpha-wave training is another concern. Equipment advertised to the public as capable of detecting alpha activity may not be sophisticated enough to do the job. Dr. Solomon Steiner of the City University of New York says that many "artifacts" can appear to be an increase in alpha-wave output. Such artifacts include blinking of the eyes, wrinkling of the forehead, or tensing of the jaw muscles. A person who believes she is emitting relaxing alpha, Dr. Steiner cautions, may be doing no more than reinforcing a tendency toward jittery eyeballs. Other scientists point out that in some people alpha waves are associated with anxiety, rather than with a feeling of well-being. If such people train themselves to produce increased alpha, the results could be unpleasant if not dangerous.

Where do these criticisms, and the others we have seen in this chapter, leave biofeedback? Was it only a fad of the 1960s and 1970s, a fad based on faulty science and on a few experiments that canot be replicated? Or is it a wonderful tool for healing, a means of making body and mind work together to enhance physical and emotional health? These are the questions that biofeedback researchers are asking, and trying to answer, today.

ASSESSING BIOFEEDBACK

Biofeedback: Issues in Treatment Assessment is the name of a booklet prepared by the National Institutes of Mental Health (NIMH). NIMH is part of the federal government's Department of Health and Human Services. Published in 1980, the booklet summarizes and critically compares twenty years' worth of biofeedback studies. It offers an overview of the science of biofeedback, its theory and practice, from initial enthusiasm to present-day questions and doubts. According to the booklet's authors, this progression from enthusiasm to skepticism is typical of many new physical or psychological treatments.

The first stage for a new treatment is the discovery stage—the Eureka state. A technique, in this case biofeedback training, is developed. There are claims of dramatic success, and more and more doctors, scientists, and researchers are drawn to the new science. More successes are reported.

Visitors to Dr. Barbara Brown's Sepulveda Veterans' Administration Hospital lab who were convinced that biofeedback was "the impossible dream" were in the grip of the Eureka feeling. So was Brown herself. "The magnitude of the future of bio-feedback was too great to allow anything else," she wrote. "Everyone was dreaming his own dream. A way to control the uncontrollable inner man, a way to know the self, a way to cure illnesses, a way to prevent illness, a way to make the mind more mindly, a way perhaps to genius."

Perhaps—and perhaps not. For as suddenly as air bursts from a pricked balloon, biofeedback's second stage commenced. This was the Show-me stage.

With this stage came doubts and questions: The samples are too small, there's too little follow-up, vital experiments cannot be replicated. Instead of carrying reports of success, the scientific journals were silent or critical. The entire technique was called into question. For biofeedback, Eureka gave way to Show-me in the early to mid-1970s.

Intrigued by the shift, Neal Miller and Barry Dworkin undertook a study of the reasons behind it. They wanted to find out why a treatment that seemed so promising at first abruptly appeared to be ineffective. The two published their findings in 1977.

In their report they pointed out that scientific journals tend to print articles about successes, not failures. Suppose three separate researchers submit papers about biofeedback. Two report that the patients gained little from the technique. The third reports positive results. Of the three, the third may be the only one to appear in print.

Furthermore, Miller and Dworkin found that journals are slow to publish papers dealing with replication attempts. Thus, other experiments that fail to confirm the findings of the published report may not be printed.

This means that readers of scientific journals are likely to see report after report about the success of a new technique. To begin with, there is little criticism. Small attention is paid to the success or failure of efforts to reproduce apparently successful experiments. The Eureka stage builds and enthusiasm mounts wildly. When the inevitable happens, and questions do begin to be asked, the shock is all the greater. The plunge into the Show-me stage is swift indeed.

If journal editors are partly to blame for this, scientists too must share the responsibility, according to Miller and Dworkin. They contend that men and women who are experimenting with a new technique are all too prone to overlook problems, such as the problem of the placebo effect. This effect, nearly always present in medicine, is particularly pronounced in experimentation with new treatments.

Why? "Often," Miller and Dworkin report, "new treatments are administered with new enthusiasm and hence produce larger placebo effects. All too often, both the enthusiasm and the effects decline." When they do, the treatment is regarded with skepticism.

However, the skeptical Show-me stage is not the end. NIMH's booklet identifies two more stages for a new medical treatment—Rebuttal and Fine-tuning. During these stages, proponents of the treatment respond to their critics. They refine their ideas and their techniques. For biofeedback, these third and fourth stages began with the 1980s.

One of the most telling criticisms of biofeedback training concerns the placebo effect. As we saw in Chapter 5, many people maintain that electrodes, wires, EEGs, EMGs—in fact, most of the equipment of biofeedback—are unnecessary, superfluous. If biofeedback is effective, they say, it is because of the attention patients get from a therapist and the care and attention they are giving to themselves.

Biofeedback enthusiasts rebut that argument, of

Supporters of biofeedback training insist that their equipment is an important part of the learning process, as is the rapport between therapist and subject.

course. They believe their equipment is essential. They also believe that the placebo effect is important. So what if their patients get better because they *think* they are getting better? That there is a placebo element in biofeedback does not mean that biofeedback does not work. The placebo effect is an intrinsic part of all medicine, biofeedback researchers tell their critics.

Dr. Miller lists some of the "cures" that doctors have tried out on their patients over the ages: "bloodletting and puking and medicines such as the eye of newt, crocodile dung, fly specks, flesh of vipers, the gound-up sole of a wornout shoe." Yet despite such repulsive-sounding remedies, "physicians nevertheless maintained their position of honor and respect." Miller and others believe that "this was possible primarily by virtue of the powerful placebo effect and the ability of the human body to produce its own recovery." In other words, placebos are neither an extraneous factor in biofeedback nor in any other kind of medical treatment. They are essential in helping the body to heal itself.

Dr. Barbara Brown agrees. She points out that 35 percent of the patients in any experimental group will improve markedly on placebos alone. "Acknowledging the reality of the placebo effect is important to the future of biofeedback," she writes. Both placebos and biofeedback are drugless and their benefits originate in the activity of the mind. The only difference is that the placebo action stems from nebulous subconscious desire; biofeedback effects are accomplished by awareness and learning." In Dr. Brown's opinion, the fact that the placebo effect is so strong in biofeedback medicine is a positive point, not a negative one.

Similar arguments are made regarding the importance of the patient–therapist relationship. Certainly biofeedback subjects do better if they like and trust the therapist who is instructing them. Virtually all patients do better if they like and trust the doctor who is giving them drugs and ordering them into the hospital, too. What is so surprising about that?

Most biofeedback researchers rebut the idea that the placebo effect and supportive patient–therapist relationships mean that biofeedback does not work in and of itself. Still, many of them agree that a great deal more basic research is needed before the technique can be widely accepted as a conventional medical tool. As Miller and Dworkin put it, the evidence for and against the workability of biofeedback is "strong enough to justify, but weak enough to require, the performance of more rigorously controlled studies."

Such studies were lacking as the 1980s began, say experts at NIMH. They must be done if biofeedback is to emerge from the fourth stage of development—the Fine-tuning stage—and become a part of the mainstream of Western medicine. Any fine-tuning studies must be designed and carried out according to strict criteria:

• *The studies must be done over sufficiently long periods of time.*

Three or four weeks is not enough time to evaluate a treatment. It is impossible to conclude, on the basis of five one-hour sessions, or one session a week for two months, that training has been successful. Yet many researchers have tried to draw such conclusions. It will be necessary to plan studies that continue for months or years.

• *The studies must involve sufficiently large samples.*

In the past, researchers have reported "success" based on the experiences of a dozen or so men and women. The reactions of hundreds—thousands—of subjects must be collected and analyzed before anyone can make definitive statements about the effectiveness of a particular treatment.

- *The studies must include follow-up reports.*

Until now, follow-up has been minimal. A person who uses biofeedback to learn to reduce hypertension in the lab does not benefit unless he or she can use that knowledge over time. Hypertension can be a lifelong problem. Researchers must be able to demonstrate that once acquired, biofeedback skills can be retained for as long as they may be needed. Otherwise, they will be useless. If biofeedback is used in place of drugs, its misuse may even be dangerous.

- *The studies must show that biofeedback skills learned in the lab are suited to use in everyday life.*

Biofeedback enthusiasts claim that the techniques they teach can be used on the job, in tense family situations, in times of crisis. Studies have yet to prove that this is true for most people.

- *The studies must rely upon objective measurement whenever possible.*

Too many biofeedback success stories depend for verification upon subjective patient report. "I feel better," or "It doesn't bother me as much." Scientists will have to design systems for more precise measurement of physical functions. At the same time, they will need to find ways to translate their measurements into accurate descriptions of physical and mental states.

- *Researchers must begin to standardize their practices and their methods of reporting results.*

Every biofeedback researcher seems to have his or her own individual way of conducting experiments and analyzing the results. That makes it nearly impossible to compare various studies, even when those studies are closely related. One researcher offers visual feedback; another uses sound. One places subjects in a darkened lab; another, in a brightly lit hospital room. One encourages her subjects; another acts more objectively. Standards of what it means to "succeed" vary from researcher to researcher. Add to these variations the patient, therapist, and time-span variables tabulated by Dr. Gordon Paul (Chapter 5) and you end up with a statistical nightmare.

• *Researchers must find ways to design double-blind tests and experiments.*

The double-blind test is a classic means of testing in medicine. Imagine that scientists want to find out how effective a new drug is. They select experimental subjects and divide them into two groups. The first group gets the drug. The second gets a placebo. In neither case do the subjects know what they are getting. Theoretically, this allows the scientists to eliminate any placebo-effect "cures."

But testing this way may not be sufficient to do so. When the scientists who are doing the testing know who is getting the drug and who is not, their reactions may affect the results. They may act enthusiastically when they are offering the genuine drug and less happy when they administer the placebo. Such attitudes may be sensed by the subjects, who will then be able to figure out whether they are getting medicine or a sugar pill. Even if the scientists strive for complete neutrality, they may not achieve it. That's why double-blind tests were devised.

In a double-blind test, neither the subject nor the experimenter knows who is getting the drug and who the placebo. Scientists believe that only with strict double-blind testing can the placebo effect be absolutely ruled out.

But can double-blind tests be designed for biofeedback studies? We have already seen that patients can sometimes tell when the researchers are feeding them false feedback signals. What if the researchers are subjected to false signals as well? The confusion in the lab could be monumental!

Confusion is not the point, but meticulous testing is. However difficult it may be to design foolproof tests and standardized procedures, it will be necessary. Biofeedback researchers must subject themselves to the fine-tuning process. If they do not, their science cannot be accepted by the medical community and by the public at large. People will remain skeptical. They will suspect that biofeedback is an unscientific mixture of placebo, "bedside manner," electronic gadgetry, and pop fad.

Yet if biofeedback researchers do put themselves through the scrutiny of the fine-tuning stage, they will be most unusual in the area of medicine. As Neal Miller pointed out, in reviewing NIMH's *Biofeedback: Issues in Treatment Assessment*: "Except for drugs, surprisingly few of the therapeutic techniques widely used by physicians have been subjected to the rigorous type of evaluation correctly called for in the case of biofeedback."

Another scientist elaborates on that: "Biofeedback is unique among all the behavioral-medical disciplines in being absolutely committed to modification of itself and its methods in response to feedback regarding . . . effectiveness in the real world."

Biofeedback feedback. That's what is needed now.

7

BIOFEEDBACK AND THE FUTURE

Picture the scene . . .

The room is decorated for a party. Music is playing. People laugh and talk. Lights flash.

But these are not ordinary lights fastened to walls or ceiling. These are lights pinned over the heart of each person in the room. Attached via an electrode to the chest, each light monitors—for all the world to see—a person's heartbeat rate.

This scene was dreamed up by Dr. Thomas Mulholland, a biofeedback researcher at the Veterans' Administration Hospital in Bedford, Massachusetts. The idea behind what he calls "heart pins" is to allow people to become better tuned in to each other's moods and feelings.

In Dr. Mulholland's imagination, a man at the party steps up to a woman. As he speaks to her, his heart pin pulses faster. The woman—assuming she likes what she sees—responds in kind. *Her* heart beats faster, too. This could really be the start of something.

Some might argue that wearing heart pins would take much of the mystery out of romance. But, says Dr. Mulholland, "it would be of great interest to discover if such procedures could teach people to have a much greater sensitivity to . . . behavior which reflects emotional states."

Heart pins are just one way biofeedback might be put to use in the future. Another suggestion put forth by Mulholland is for utilizing the technique to help diagnose brain disorders. Dr. Joe Kamiya, the alpha-wave researcher, applauds this proposal. "Someday it might be possible to examine a patient's physiological states and diagnose his neurosis," Kamiya believes. Using biofeedback this way, he says, would be little different from the way "the physician now detects tuberculosis by examining an X-ray."

Barbara Brown is convinced that biofeedback will become a way of life for Americans. "In five years," she wrote, "there will be biofeedback centers all over the country, in which people can learn all manner of mind and body functions."

Dr. Brown made that prediction in 1971. It did not come true. Nor is it likely to come true in the near future. There are still too many questions about biofeedback and what it can accomplish.

That it can accomplish some things is accepted by most doctors and scientists. The disagreement is over how much it can do, and how it gets its effects.

So far, biofeedback's greatest area of medical success seems to lie in helping the paralyzed or partially paralyzed and those with movement disorders. As we have seen, people with tics or with cerebral palsy and victims of stroke or accident have been among those whose conditions have improved after biofeedback training.

Even many critics concede the technique's usefulness in this area. According to NIMH, biofeedback's results have been "impressive in view of the fact that virtually all the patients [in studies that have been done] had failed to respond to conventional forms of physical therapy." Still, more studies are needed, the critics agree. Biofeedback training to regain movement, they conclude, "offers new hope but no miracles."

Beyond treatment of movement disorders, questions about biofeedback multiply. "The case for the clinical effectiveness of biofeedback is still open," the authors of NIMH's *Biofeedback* conclude. Some biofeedback researchers concur. According to two participants at a 1976 conference on the subject, "Biofeedback . . . may play some part in the study of man and in the treatment of human disorders. That part may not be large, but in selected areas it may be important."

Some think that its importance may be not so much as a means of treating specific illnesses but as a path toward changing the way twentieth-century Americans think about themselves and their health.

The biofeedback revolution has given people new ideas about how their minds and bodies work together in sickness and in health. No longer must people think of their bodies as something totally outside their conscious control. Today we know that people can use their minds to affect body processes.

How people accomplish that is another matter. It may be because electrodes have been placed on parts of their bodies. It may be because they are wired to machines. It may be because they are relaxed, or because the therapist is pleasant, or because of the placebo effect. It may be because a kind of self-hypnosis or faith healing occurs. It may be because of a combination of several factors—or none of them.

The "becauses" are not the point. The point is that people can use their minds to alter what is going on in their bodies at least some of the time. And that means that medicine faces a revolution of its own.

Knowing that our minds affect how our bodies function makes people, as individuals, more responsible for their own health. It makes every person an active partner in maintaining good health and in battling illness.

Writing in the *New York Times Magazine*, Gay Luce and Erik Peper hail biofeedback's promise "to return us to a more holistic kind of medicine in which the patient will . . . no longer [find] himself treated as a defective organ, but as a person in a context with a lifestyle and habits that affect his own body."

Biofeedback training—fact or fad? We do not yet know for sure. One thing is certain, though. The study of biofeedback has opened new windows for Western science, Western medicine.

Biofeedback research has provided valuable information on ways the body and mind can work together.

FOR FURTHER READING

Brown, Barbara B., *New Mind, New Body*. Harper & Row, New York, 1974.

Green, Elmer, and Alyce Green, *Beyond Biofeedback*. Dell, New York, 1977.

Jonas, Gerald, *Visceral Learning: Toward a Science of Self-control*. Viking, New York, 1972.

Karlins, Marvin, and Lewis M. Andrews, *Biofeedback: Turning on the Power of Your Mind*. Lippincott, Philadelphia, 1972.

Science Reports, *Biofeedback: Issues in Treatment Assessment*. National Institutes of Mental Health, Rockville, Md., 1980.

Weiss, Malcolm E., *The World Within the Brain*. Messner, New York, 1974.

INDEX

Proprioception, 32
Psychophysiology, 23
Punishment, 18

Rebuttal stage, 67
Replication, 49, 51–54
Respiration, 11, 42, 44
Rewards, 18–20

Salivation, 18
Self-treatment, 63–64
Show-me stage, 66, 67
Sight, 10
Skinner, B.F., 16
Sleep, 43
Smell, 10
Stroke victims, 32
Stuttering, 35
Subconscious mind, 43
Subvocalization, 34–35

Taste, 10

Taub, Edward, 56, 58
Temperature, body, 23–24,
    27, 33, 46, 56
Theta, 38, 39, 43
Tics, 1–2
Tinnitus, 34
Touch, 10
Trance, 46

Ulcers, 32–33, 42

Voluntary nervous system,
    11, 18–21, 52–53

Wandering eye, *31*
Western science, 11–21,
    44, 46

Yogis, 11–12, 21, 44, *45*,
    46

Zen, 46

ABOUT THE AUTHOR

Anne E. Weiss was born in Newton, Massachusetts, and was educated at Brown University. She is well-known as an author of nonfiction books for young people, several of which have won awards and have been recognized as Outstanding Trade Books by the National Council for the Social Studies and the National Science Teachers Association. She is the author of the Franklin Watts books *Polls and Surveys: A Look at Public Opinion Research,* and *Over-the-Counter Drugs.* Ms. Weiss lives with her husband, Malcolm E. Weiss, and their two daughters in North Whitefield, Maine.